Contemplations On The Ashtavakra Gita of Shri Ashtavakra

By Kedarji

Contemplations On
The Ashtavakra Gita of
Shri Ashtavakra

Copies of this book may be ordered by contacting:
The Bhakta School of Transformation, Inc.
330-623-7388 Ext. 10
NityanandaShaktipatYoga.org

ISBN: 979-8-218-74239-3

Printed in the United States of America

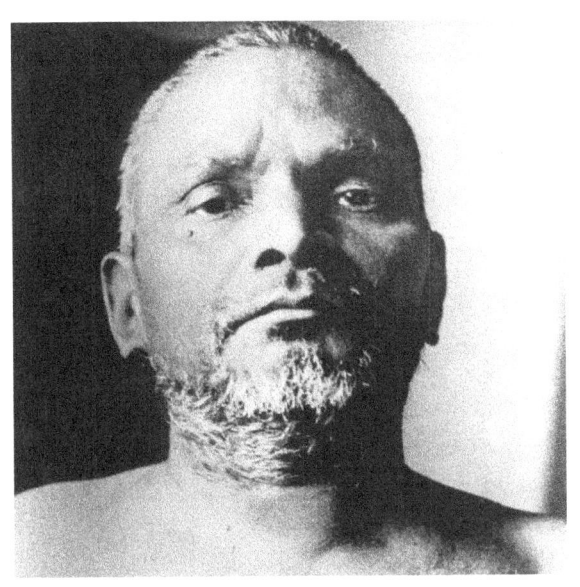

Shri Bhagawan Nityananda of Ganeshpuri
The Master of Kedarji's Lineage

Contents

Introduction

Acknowledgement is offered to John Richards whose translation of the Ashtavakra Gita has inspired this work.

My Shri Gurudev, Muktananda Paramahamsa offered lessons from the wisdom utterances of Ashtavakra and told his story. Ashtavakra is considered to be one of the greatest Siddhas to have ever graced this planet.

Ashtavakra means deformed in eight places. The sage Aruni ran an ashram in which the Vedas were taught. Kahoḍa, Ashtavakra's father, was one of his students, along with Aruni's daughter Sujata. Aruni's daughter married Kahoḍa. She got pregnant, and during her pregnancy, the unborn baby (Ashtavakra) heard the chanting of the Vedas and learned the correct recitation.

According to one version of the legends surrounding Ashtavakra, his father, Kahoda, was reciting the Vedas one day, but incorrectly. The fetus (Ashtavakra) spoke from the womb and told his father that he was not reciting the mantras correctly. Kahoda got angry and cursed him to be born with eight deformities, hence the name Ashtavakra.

Ashtavakra and King Janaka

King Janaka was a mogul king with a large army. One evening, Janaka had a vivid dream that frightened him. He dreamt that he was a beggar who has gone without food for 15 days. As this beggar, he finally found a shelter but it was closing for the day, just as he arrived.

Standing at the gate of the shelter, dying of hunger, he begged that the bowl from which food had just been distributed be scraped and the scraps given to him. One of the attendants standing at the gate did this and gave him a little bit of spiced vegetable in a tin plate.

The beggar staggered across the street into a field and sat down to eat his tiny portion. In that same field there were two bulls fighting. Upon seeing him, one of the bulls charged him and tossed the food up in the air, scattering it everywhere. Just at that moment, finding himself in a state of horror, his eyes opened to find that he was, in fact, King Janaka lying in his royal bed, being fanned by hi queens.

Closing his eyes again, he found himself to be the beggar sitting in the field, confronted by that bull. When he opened his eyes again, he was the king.

King Janaka became obsessed with this dream. Who was he? The king or the beggar? Was the identity of one more real than the other? So, Janaka issued a proclamation that all the great sages and sadhus in his kingdom should be summoned to his court to interpret his dream. When none of them could interpret his dream, the king had them all imprisoned.

One of those imprisoned was Kahoda, Ashtavakra's father. When he Ashtavakra that his father was in the king's jail, immediately he set out to King Janaka's court.

When Ashtavakra entered Janaka's court, upon seeing his deformities and the jerking way in which he moved, all those in the court began to laugh hysterically at him. To their astonishment, Ashtavakra himself began to laugh out loud, whereupon a sudden hush came over the entire court.

Who are you boy? And what are you laughing at, asked Janaka. Ashtavakra replied, "I have heard such great things about you King Janaka, and the splendor of your court. But now I see that you are all just a pack of leather merchants. You look a me and you only see the external skin and deformity of my body. You are blind to that spirit that animates it. Now, ask your question so that my father can go free."

Astonished at Ashtavakra's authority and spiritual radiance, the king explained his dream. Ashtavakra said, "King, when you are a beggar in your dream, being a king is not a reality for you. And when you are a king, being a beggar is not a reality. In fact, neither identity is real. Reality is that from which both identities are projected — the pure, the absolute witness, the Self."

King Janaka's confusion vanished. His mind was illuminated with the light of the Self and he became the disciple of Ashtavakra.

The Ashtavakra Gita is a recording of the instruction of Shri Ashtavakra, given to us all, by way of his instruction to King Janaka.

About the Author

Kedarji is the Founder of The Bhakta School of Transformation, an Ohio-based not-for-profit public charity devoted to lasting Inner Peace and permanent spiritual transformation. The curriculum offered here is based on Kedaji's *4 Pillars of Joy In Daily Living*.

He had an early career in the Performing Arts as an actor and singer in Broadway musicals, plays, movies and television. He went on to study violin and conducting at the Juilliard School of Music and graduated with degrees in performance and composition from the Manhattan School of Music. Later, he studied Eastern and Oriental Medicine, graduated with degrees in both from the Kushi Institute, and had a practice in New York City for many years.

Leading With Love

Kedarji helps people embrace the Grace in life's joys and challenges in a way that causes lasting happiness and peace. In a world seemingly mad with greed and corruption, Kedarji has a long track record of helping people affirm and expand the best parts of their lives.

He is a Sadhu in the lineage of the great sage and saint, Bhagawan Nityananda of Ganeshpuri. He imparts the same instruction and leadership he was taught— the same methods used by a line of spiritually proven and powerful masters who have uplifted people's lives for thousands of years.

A Sadhu is one who has made the commitment to live as an ascetic, renouncing the pursuit of worldly pleasures and fantasies to serve the greater good and to work to uplift humanity. In this regard, Kedarji is also known as a Sadguru, meaning true spiritual leader, and a Shaktipat Guru (see below) who leads by example in becoming both wise and well with a powerful, heart-centered approach.

Practical Leadership
In A Shaktipat Guru

Kedarji has a reputation for leading without insisting that people follow. This allows students and seekers to come to our approach in their own way. For Kedarji, the reference to Sadguru is a reference to our lineage of Siddha Gurus on whose shoulders he stands and takes refuge in. This is the great Shiva lineage that Bhagawan Nityananda of Ganeshpuri also made, of which Kedarji is a part.

Wise, Happy and Well

Many of Kedarji's students say that, through his leadership, he has transformed their lives in profound ways not experienced in other modalities or on other paths.

His students blossom and uncover hidden strengths through a well-integrated and time-tested approach. Through his leadership, it's possible for anyone and everyone to experience life's magic in a way that they come to know their true nature and attain a state of lasting happiness, peace and joy.

With his 4 Pillars of Joy In Daily Living as the foundation (the Spiritual Power, Improved Mental State, Emotional Resilience and Vibrant Health), he combines the power of Grace of his spiritual lineage with the time-honored, Siddha Science of the Yoga of the Siddhas. This powerful combination includes his skill as a Shaktipat Meditation master.

Authentic Shaktipat Guru – Shaktipat Meditation Master

Kedarji is a Shaktipat Guru. He has been vested with the power and authority to fully awaken and nurture the dormant spiritual awareness known as Kundalini. Specifically, this awakening occurs by way of the transmission of the Grace-bestowing power inherent in the Blessing of Shaktipat. In particular, you will find that Kedarji is a recognized and very skilled spiritual leader and Shaktipat Meditation Master. Additionally, his is the ability to lead you on the journey to the realization of your true nature or Self-Realization. Indeed, this is a journey in which you retrace your steps back to God.

Author/Producer

Kedarji is the author of several books and courses, including:

- Vibration of Divine Consciousness. A Spiritual Autobiography.
- The Verses On Witness Consciousness.

- The Abode of Grace. Bhagawan Nityananda of Ganeshpuri.
- How To Be Fearless, Happy and Resilient In The Age of Noise and Distractions (a video home-study course and weekend retreat).
- The Sutras On The 5-Fold Act of Divine Consciousness.
- Live Strong and Be Happy. Learn The Daily Rituals of The Most Spiritually-Powerful, Happiest and Healthiest People On The Planet.
- Contemplations On the Amritanubhava of Shri Jnaneshwar Maharaj.
- Dharma and the Preservation of Liberty. The Globalist Threat to Our Freedom and What to Do About It.
- The Courage To Love.
- Your Inner State Is Your Fate.
- Shaktipat - The Miracle of Grace. Authentic Shaktipat, Who Can Give It, The Benefits of Receiving It.

Spiritual Journey

Kedarji began his quest to understand and fully imbibe Yoga Science at an early age. Feeling incomplete, Kedarji began an intense spiritual journey that took him to India and Asia. Soon after, he experienced an initiation, an awakening into the power of true Meditation, Chanting and Contemplation that formed the foundation for putting all the pieces together.

Due to this event and ongoing application of the methods taught connected to it, Kedarji was able to fully apply the science behind well-being that is based on the Spiritual Power. He calls it the energy substratum of everything. His direct, unfolding experience of this power is the basis for the integration of his 4 Pillars of Joy In Daily Living embodied in his unique approach: An approach that combines Siddha Science and the science of a holistic lifestyle of health and well-being with the transmission of Grace that he extends as a God-realized, Shaktipat Guru.

How to Use the Contemplations

In this book, the words "the Supreme," "the Atman," "the Self," "Consciousness" and "God" are used interchangeably and are all references to the formless Absolute, the One God.

These contemplations have manifested out of many years of offering lessons on the Ashtavakra Gita in programs and courses. Each is designed to be contemplated and not just merely to be read.

To contemplate means to steadily regard with your heart, without prejudging or forming premature notions about that which you are contemplating. It is best to perform each contemplation inwardly in silence for approximately 3-4 minutes. While performing a contemplation, observe what you experience inside, along with the state of your mind and any inner shifts in your awareness and inner state.

It is best to record in a journal whatever you experience and observe as you perform each contemplation. A specific contemplation can be performed more than once. The contemplations do not have to be performed in any particular sequence or order, and you can start wherever you like.

Journaling your observations and inner experiences is very useful.

Chapter 1

King Janaka Asks a Question of Ashtavakra: How is knowledge to be acquired? How is liberation to be attained? And how is dispassion to be reached? Tell me this, sir.

The following contemplations are based on Ashtavakra's answer to these questions.

Contemplation 1
To attain liberation from the ignorance of worldliness, attachment to objects of sense must be destroyed. When this attachment is broken, the practice of tolerance, sincerity, compassion, contentment and truthfulness is an easy matter that brings the experience of Joy.

Contemplation 2
You are not the mind, the body or the senses. Neither are you any of the earthly elements. You are that Consciousness that is the eternal witness to these. Understanding this, become liberated from the bondage of worldliness.

Contemplation 3
If you become absorbed in that Consciousness, the inner Self, you will come to know that you are not just a person, and that you are not the body, the mind or the senses. Then you will be happy, peaceful and free from all bonds.

Contemplation 4
You do not belong to any nation, race or creed.

Nor are you anything that the eye can see. You are the observer of all there is, the eternal witness to everything, the formless Absolute. So, be happy.

Contemplation 5
Pleasure and pain are of the mind only and are no concern of yours. You are not the doer nor the possessor of outcomes, so you are always free.

Contemplation 6
You are that witness to your mind, the supreme Observer of everything and everyone. This means you are always free. The cause of your bondage is that you think you are something other than this.

Contemplation 7
You have come to believe that you, as the mind, body and the senses are the doer - that you have the right to possess people, places and things to some degree. Experience God inside you. Then you will come to know that you are not the doer, and you will be happy.

Contemplation 8
Free yourself from the bondage of the ego with the highest understanding "I am that pure, spiritual witnessing awareness, the observer of all that is," and be joyful and free from fear.

Contemplation 9
Nothing exists that is outside of Consciousness. This entire world-appearance is imagined. You are the supreme awareness and indescribable Joy of the Self. So, be happy.

Contemplation 10
Understanding, based on experience, is
everything. If you know you are God, the inner
Self, you are free. If you don't know this, you are
bound. A quiet mind, free of restlessness, is
essential to freedom.

Contemplation 11
Your natural, free state of being is that of
perfection, freedom, and actionless
Consciousness, the all-pervading Witness. This
witness is unattached to anything, desireless and
at peace. Due to the illusion of worldly existence,
you appear to be small and bound when, in fact,
you are the boundless, eternal Self.

Contemplation 12
Meditate on the Self with the understanding that
you are motionless awareness, free from any
dualism. Give up the mistaken idea that you are
just a person, just the mind, body and senses.

Contemplation 13
You have long been trapped in the prison of
identity as an individual. Open the prison gate
with the key of knowledge that "I am That - the
Supreme Self," and be happy.

Contemplation 14
You are not an individual, bound soul. You are
the actionless Observer, the inner Self that is
spotless. The cause of your bondage is that you
are stuck in the notion that you and God are
separate.

Contemplation 15
The entire world exists inside you and you
pervade all objects of sense (people, places and

things). You are That - the Pure Perceiving Awareness of the One God. So, don't be small-minded.

Contemplation 16
You are the formless, changeless, unconditioned One. You are the immovable, unperturbed Self. That Self alone exists. Hold to That and nothing else.

Contemplation 17
Realize that the world of forms is imaginary, while the Shiva-Shakti power that is the cause of manifestation of forms is alone what is real. By embracing this truth, you will escape the prison of worldliness.

Contemplation 18
Just as a mirror reflects images within it but is also the cause of those reflections, the body is reflected in the Supreme Lord who exists everywhere and is the cause of the reflection of the body.

Contemplation 19
Just as all-pervading space exists inside and outside of a jar, so the eternal, everlasting God exists in the totality of all things.

Chapter 2

Ashtavakra's wisdom has pierced the veil of King Janaka's ignorance, and Janaka shares his realization of the Truth. The following contemplations are based on that.

Contemplation 20
Truly I am spotless and at peace. I am the pure, witnessing awareness beyond forms. All this time I have been afflicted by delusion.

Contemplation 21
I am the Light that gives life to this body. I am that same Light of the world. As a result the whole world is mine, or alternatively nothing is.

Contemplation 22
When I abandon my attachment to the body and all other people, places and things, my true nature as the Self becomes apparent.

Contemplation 23
Just as the waves of the ocean are water only, so all this which has emanated from God is nothing other than God. It is all the play of the Shakti as this world.

Contemplation 24
In the same way, just as cloth is just thread, when observed closely and properly understood, all this is nothing other than the Shakti that has caused all this to manifest.

Contemplation 25
I am That. Just as sugarcane produces the taste of sugar, this entire world is manifest out of me and is permeated by me.

Contemplation 26
The notion that this world is separate and apart from God is ignorance. By direct knowledge and experience of the Self, this world no longer appears as separate and apart from God. God alone is.

Contemplation 27
From ignorance of my true nature, the world appears to be real and separate from me. By direct knowledge and experience of my true nature, I know that there is no outer world and that God alone exists. I am That.

Contemplation 28
Because shining (manifestation) is my essential nature, when the world shines forth, it is simply me that is shining forth.

Contemplation 29
In fact, this entire world-appearance is reflected in me and is imaginary, just as the mirage of the moon reflected in water on a bright, clear night.

Contemplation 30
All this has originated out of me and is withdrawn back into me - like a clay jug back into clay, a wave into water, and a gold bracelet into gold.

Contemplation 31
I am God and God is me! Glory to me who pervades everything and everyone, for whom

there is no destruction (withdrawal). I remain even when the world is withdrawn.

Contemplation 32
I am That, wonderful and glorious! Even though I inhabit a body, I neither come or go anywhere. I abide in all that is and all that is not.

Contemplation 33
I am That, wonderful and glorious! I am both the cause and the effect of everything. I exist without beginning and without end.

Contemplation 34
I am That, wonderful and glorious! I who possess nothing at all, or alternatively possess everything that speech and mind can refer to.

Contemplation 35
Knowledge, what is to be known, and the knower are one and the same. These are experienced at one point inside the body of Supreme Consciousness. This is the proof that there is no outer world.

Contemplation 36
The notions of duality and diversity are the root cause of all suffering. The only remedy is the realization that God alone is real, and that the objects (people, places and things) of this world are imaginary. Or it can be understood that these objects are expressions of the One God.

Contemplation 37
I am the pure perceiving awareness that expresses itself through what appears to be attributes. These attributes are my illusion. In fact, I dwell in the Unimagined.

Contemplation 38
For me here is neither bondage nor liberation. Both are an illusion that dissolves in contact with the Self. Truly all this exists in me, though ultimately all this is imaginary because God alone exists.

Contemplation 39
I recognize that everything in form is a reflection of the inner Self. And I am That – the inner Self of all.

Contemplation 40
People, places and things are imaginary. I am the Reality from which these manifest. This is the supreme realization.

Contemplation 41
I see only God in everything and everyone, everywhere. Therefore, I have no need to run away from this world-appearance.

Contemplation 42
I am not the body, nor the mind or the senses. I am the formless Absolute from which these manifest. It was my thirst for worldliness that caused me to be bound.

Contemplation 43
The universe of all the worlds arises in me, is sustained by me and is withdrawn by me. I am That by whose power all things come into being.

Contemplation 44
It is in the limitless ocean of my Self, the body of Supreme Consciousness that thoughts come and go, like clouds in the sky. All this dissolves in the indescribable Joy of the Self.

Contemplation 45
How wonderful it is that in the limitless ocean –
the body of Supreme Consciousness – all people,
places and things manifest, are sustained and
then withdrawn, according to their natures.

Chapter 3

Ashtavakra continues to share his wisdom and instruction. The following contemplations are based on that instruction.

Contemplation 46
Knowing yourself as That, the Self, without beginning or end, you are indestructible. With this Self-knowledge there is no need to pursue comfort, security and reward.

Contemplation 47
If you don't know who you are – that you are God, you will become whoever and whatever others want you to be. And you will take pleasure and pride in your contraction.

Contemplation 48
This world-appearance rises inside the body of Supreme Consciousness as an expression of That. Recognizing, "I am That" why run around like someone in need?

Contemplation 49
After coming to know your inner Self and after experiencing the indescribable Joy of the Self, what need is there for lusting after worldly pleasures?

Contemplation 50
When you realize that God exists equally in everything and everyone, everywhere, and that all beings are contained in you, and you in all beings, the false notion of individuality ceases.

Contemplation 51
Upon reaching the supreme non-dual state of Liberation, a person is no longer subject to lust, nor does such a person pursue sexual activity.

Contemplation 52
The unenlightened further debilitate themselves by pursuing sensuality, even when approaching their final days.

Contemplation 53
One can long for Liberation and still be afraid of it, even when the mind has become quieter and discernment increases. This is due to the existence of the limitation of the ego which can only be rooted out by the Grace and leadership of a Sadguru.

Contemplation 54
A wise person is one who is always aware of his identity as the Supreme Self, regardless of circumstance. Such a being remains unattached to people, places and things while reveling in the indescribable Joy of the Self.

Contemplation 55
Experiencing that it is God who occupies the body, a Liberated being is undisturbed by praise and blame.

Contemplation 56
Understanding this world-appearance to be imaginary, a yogi becomes fearless, even at the approach of death.

Contemplation 57
There is nothing greater than direct knowledge and experience of the Self. The indescribable Joy

of the Self destroys limiting desire and craving, even in disappointment, and eliminates expectations of outcomes.

Contemplation 58
One who understands this world-appearance as the play of the Shakti as this world and relishes in the Self knows that there is no such thing as gain or loss. Attachment and aversion cannot touch such a being.

Contemplation 59
If pleasurable things come your way, unsought, enjoy them. But never go looking. This is the means to free yourself from the false notions of duality and diversity, and to eliminate limiting desire and craving for this and that.

Chapter 4

Ashtavakra's wisdom has pierced the veil of King Janaka's ignorance, and Janaka continues to share his realization of the Truth. The following contemplations are based on that.

Contemplation 60
Those absorbed in the Self play at their various roles, recognizing all as a play of the Shakti. Such a being is not bound by the samsara of this world.

Contemplation 61
When you remain absorbed in the indescribable Joy of the Self, the highest state of Vairagya, elated dispassion dawns.

Contemplation 62
When you know That, you are untouched by what appears to be 'good' or 'bad' deeds, just as the sky is not touched by smoke, however much smoke may appear to be.

Contemplation 63
When you come to know the entire world as your very own Self, you can live as you please.

Contemplation 64
Of all four categories of beings, from Brahma down to the last clump of grass, only the one who knows the Self can eliminate attachment and aversion.

Contemplation 65

Rare is the one who knows himself as the undivided Lord of the world and, coming to know this, is fearless.

Chapter 5

Ashtavakra continues to share his wisdom and instruction. The following contemplations are based on that instruction.

Contemplation 66
In truth, you are the One God and are not bound by anything. Therefore, there is nothing to accept and nothing to renounce. Rest in the knowledge of That.

Contemplation 67
All this arises out of you, like a bubble out of the sea. Knowing that you are one with God, rest in the knowledge of That.

Contemplation 68
You are spotless. All that you experience in this world-appearance is a prolonged dream – a play of the Shakti. Rest in the knowledge of That.

Contemplation 69
Unmoved by pain or pleasure, unmoved by hope or disappointment, unmoved by life or death, one in the Self, rest in the knowledge of That.

Chapter 6

Upon hearing the utterances of Ashtavakra, Janaka continues to share his realization of the Truth. The following contemplations are based on that.

Contemplation 70
I am infinite, beyond space and time. This world-appearance is but a speck within my Consciousness. The direct experience of this fact is true knowledge that renders renunciation, acceptance and rejection unnecessary.

Contemplation 71
I am the ocean of Supreme Consciousness, and the multiplicity of objects are waves that come and go on the surface of that ocean. The direct experience of this fact is true knowledge that renders renunciation, acceptance and rejection unnecessary.

Contemplation 72
This world-appearance is imagined. The people, places and things in it are reflections of the Self, my true nature. The direct experience of this fact is true knowledge that renders renunciation, acceptance and rejection unnecessary.

Contemplation 73
I am in all beings, and all beings are in me. The direct experience of this fact is true knowledge that renders renunciation, acceptance and rejection unnecessary.

Chapter 7

Upon hearing the utterances of Ashtavakra, Janaka continues to share his realization of the Truth. The following contemplations are based on that.

Contemplation 74
In the body of Supreme Consciousness that I am, this world appears and disappears, sustained for a time by my Shakti power. I am unmoved by this.

Contemplation 75
Let the world manifest, be sustained and then withdrawn within the body of Supreme Consciousness that I am. I neither gain nor lose anything by that.

Contemplation 76
It is within the body of Supreme Consciousness that I am that this entire world-appearance is reflected on the internal screen of the mind. Even so, I am supremely peaceful and formless, and I remain as such.

Contemplation 77
My true nature is not contained in objects, even though all objects are reflected in me. I am spotless, desireless, free and at peace, and I remain as such.

Contemplation 78
Truly I am pure Consciousness, and the world is

a play of my Shakti. So, there is nothing to accept or reject.

Chapter 8

Ashtavakra continues to share his wisdom and instruction. The following contemplations are based on that instruction.

Contemplation 79
Bondage occurs due to the restless mind that is consumed by limiting desire and craving for this and that. Such a mind is bounced back and forth between pleasure and pain, attachment and aversion.

Contemplation 80
Liberation is the state in which the mind is quiet, unattached to outcomes and unperturbed by praise and blame or pleasure and pain.

Contemplation 81
Bondage occurs when the restless mind attaches itself to the senses, believing sensory experience to be sought after. Liberation occurs when the mind is not tangled up in any of the senses and, instead, views sensory experience passively as an observer.

Contemplation 82
When there is no false identity of being just the mind, body and senses that is Liberation. When there is the limited false identity of being just a person, just the mind, body and senses that is bondage. Consider this carefully, and neither hold on to or reject anything.

Chapter 9

Ashtavakra continues to share his wisdom and instruction. The following contemplations are based on that instruction.

Contemplation 83
When the notions of duality and diversity are destroyed in the direct knowledge and experience of the Self, and when you come to know that God alone exists, then there is no need for renunciation and you make weeping weep.

Contemplation 84
Such a person is rare whose knowledge of this world-appearance leads to the extinction of attachment to worldliness. Become that rare being.

Contemplation 85
This world-appearance is impermanent and filled with the pursuit of pleasure in an attempt to avoid pain. Recognizing this fact and pursuing neither one attains peace.

Contemplation 86
Worldliness is steeped in the false notions of duality and diversity. It has always been this way. If you abandon these notions and accept that which comes to you unsought, you will attain perfection.

Contemplation 87
To attain peace, you must reach the state of elated dispassion. In this state there is no

perception of differences. God alone is perceived in everything and everyone, everywhere.

Contemplation 88
A Sadguru (true Guru) is endowed with dispassion and equanimity. Such a being embodies the full knowledge of the highest non-dualism and is able to free others from the dross of worldliness.

Contemplation 89
If you would just see the entire phantasmagorical existence of this world as a play of the Shakti of the Supreme, then you will immediately be freed from all bonds and established in your own God nature.

Contemplation 90
Your compulsions are due to the endless cycle of birth and death, your karmas. Knowing this, abandon limiting desire and craving, along with attachment and aversion. Renouncing these, you can remain as you are.

Chapter 10

Ashtavakra continues to share his wisdom and instruction. The following contemplations are based on that instruction.

Contemplation 91
Abandon limiting desire and craving, along with the notion of gain which is itself so full of loss. And abandon the good deeds which are the cause of the other three. Practice non-attachment to everything.

Contemplation 92
Understand that such things as friends, land, money, property, husband, wife, and possessions are all part of a prolonged dream that is short-lived.

Contemplation 93
Understand your limiting desires and cravings to be the result of your karmas, your repeated cycles of birth and death. Become established in Vairagya – elated dispassion – and be happy.

Contemplation 94
Bondage is limiting desire and craving that causes your attachment to people, places and things. When you are free of this attachment and free of aversion, that is Liberation which is the state of indescribable Joy.

Contemplation 95

You are the Self, conscious and pure. Your existence in this world of forms is a play of the Shakti. Even ignorance is an imaginary part of that play. So, what else is there to understand about Liberation?

Contemplation 96
For so many lifetimes you have been attached to people, places and things – chasing after pleasure in an attempt to avoid pain – pursuing comfort, security and reward.

Contemplation 97
And yet, through these pursuits your mind has never found satisfaction. Desire can never quench desire and only leads to more desiring.

Contemplation 98
Believing yourself to be just the mind, the body and the senses, you have embraced the roller coaster of pleasure and pain for so many births. At last now stop!

Chapter 11

Ashtavakra continues to share his wisdom and instruction. The following contemplations are based on that instruction.

Contemplation 99
Unmoved, without distress, realizing that everything here and beyond is a play of the Shakti, you easily find peace.

Contemplation 100
At peace, having shed all limiting desire and craving, and realizing that God alone exists, you are no longer attached to anything or anyone.

Contemplation 101
Realizing that misfortune and fortune are borne of your karmas that you have created, remain content and detached from sensory experience.

Contemplation 102
Realizing that pleasure and pain, birth and death are borne of the karmas you have created and realizing that desire can never quench desire and all your desires will never be fulfilled, remain unattached, even as you engage in activity.

Contemplation 103
Realizing all suffering arises from the way you think, if you abandon limiting desire and craving you will remain happy and at peace.

Contemplation 104
Realize that you are not the body, the mind or

the senses. Then you will understand that you are Pure Perceiving Awareness. You will attain the supreme state in which you no longer remember things done or undone.

Contemplation 105
Realizing, "I alone exist, from Brahma down to the last clump of grass," you become free from uncertainty, pure, at peace and unconcerned about what has been attained or not.

Contemplation 106
Realize that all this varied and wonderful world is a play of the Shakti. Then you will become pure receptivity, free from inclinations, and you will find peace.

Chapter 12

Upon hearing the utterances of Ashtavakra, Janaka continues to share his realization of the Truth. The following contemplations are based on that.

Contemplation 107
I am unattached to physical activity, I refrain from lengthy speech, and I observe my thinking passively. This is how I am now established in the Self.

Contemplation 108
I do not delight in the activity of the senses but, instead, observe that activity passively. I am not an object of the senses. Therefore, my mind is focused and free from distraction. This is how I am now established in the Self.

Contemplation 109
I relinquish the notions of acceptance and rejection and, with the cessation of the notions of pleasure and pain I am now established in the Self.

Contemplation 110
Going beyond attachment to people, places and things, I have seen the error of worldliness. This is how I am now established in the Self.

Contemplation 111
I now surrender the false notion that I, as the body, mind and senses, with a given name and

form am the doer. I am That, the One God – the only doer, the cause and effect of everything. By fully realizing this Truth, I am now established in the Self.

Contemplation 112
By reining in my restless mind and embracing the means to experience the indescribable Joy of the Self, I am now established in the Self.

Contemplation 113
The being who has achieved this direct knowledge and experience of the Self attains the goal of life. Such a being has done what has to be done.

Chapter 13

Upon hearing the utterances of Ashtavakra, Janaka continues to share his realization of the Truth. The following contemplations are based on that.

Contemplation 114
Freedom from attachment and aversion is not easily achieved. With the Grace and Blessings of a Siddha Guru, you are able to attain this freedom and you are able to abandon the notions of gain and loss. Abandoning these is renunciation.

Contemplation 115
Abandon the distress of the body. Abandon the distress of the restless mind. Abandon the distress of speech. Abandoning all of these, dwell in the glory of the Self while keeping your Humanity.

Contemplation 116
By attaining the state of Vairagya, elated dispassion, you become elated at being non-attached. Then you will recognize that, when you surrender your will to God's Will, in reality, no action is ever committed and you are able to follow God's will for your existence here.

Contemplation 117
If you identify with being just the body, the mind and the senses, you will wind up in the prison of attachment and aversion. Realize your God nature and abandon these.

Contemplation 118
Whether standing or sitting, walking, speaking or
lying down, regardless of the activity, a yogi
should remain absorbed in the indescribable Joy
of the Self. Then there is no taint.

Contemplation 119
Abandoning all notions of gain and loss, remain
absorbed in the indescribable Joy of the Self.
Then there is no taint.

Contemplation 120
In pleasure, there is always some pain and in
pain, there is always some pleasure. Abandoning
both pleasure and pain remain absorbed in the
indescribable Joy of the Self. Then there is no
taint.

Contemplation 121
Observe how your pursuit of pleasure in an
attempt to avoid pain causes you to contract in
the bondage of worldliness. Abandon this pursuit
and remain absorbed in the indescribable Joy of
the Self. Then there is no taint.

Chapter 14

Upon hearing the utterances of Ashtavakra, Janaka continues to share his realization of the Truth. The following contemplations are based on that.

Contemplation 122
The one who forgets everything and remains content in the Self is freed from the bondage of worldliness, like one awakened from a dream.

Contemplation 123
Abandon limiting desire and craving. Then you will experience that God alone exists.

Contemplation 124
Realize your supreme nature as the Witness of all that is. Then you will understand that where there is no bondage, there is no liberation either. This is the state of desirelessness.

Contemplation 125
Be free of uncertainty, fear, doubt, worry and cynicism. Then wherever you go and whatever you do, you will see your very own Self in the play of the Shakti as this world.

Chapter 15

Ashtavakra continues to share his wisdom and instruction. The following contemplations are based on that instruction.

Contemplation 126
A person who follows the instruction of a Siddha Guru may attain the goal of complete absorption in God, even by the most casual of instruction. A person without such a Guru can seek this knowledge of the Self all his life and still remain bewildered.

Contemplation 127
Liberation is non-attachment to the objects of the senses (people, places and things). Bondage is attachment to the senses. Therefore, become free of attachment to the senses and sensory experience.

Contemplation 128
The awareness of this truth makes a worldly person free from attachment to worldliness. Those attached to worldliness remain ignorant and unaware and unable to experience the Joy of the inner Self.

Contemplation 129
You are not the body, the mind or the senses. You are not the doer, and outcomes do not belong to you. You are eternally pure consciousness, the witness to all. So, be happy.

Contemplation 130
Limiting desire and craving, anger, fear doubt, worry – these are expressions of the limitation of the ego. You are not that ego, you are the supreme Self. So, be happy.

Contemplation 131
You are in all and all are in you. Therefore, discard notions of "I" and "mine," "you" and "yours" and be happy.

Contemplation 132
You are that Consciousness in which the whole world wells. This is the truth. So, be happy.

Contemplation 133
Have faith and trust in God. Do not become deluded by egoism. You are God. Your very nature is Bliss. You are beyond both cause and effect.

Contemplation 134
The body comes and goes. But you are not the body, nor the mind or the senses. You are that which gives power to these, and yet you are beyond these.

Contemplation 135
Let the body last to the end of the Age or let it come to an end right now. You gain or lose nothing by this because you consist of pure Consciousness without beginning or end.

Contemplation 136
The entire world-appearance rises and subsides within the body of Supreme Consciousness that you are. Nothing can be added to That and nothing can be taken away from That.

Contemplation 137
You consist of pure Consciousness, and the world
is contained inside you. There is nothing to
accept or reject.

Contemplation 138
Birth, death and the suffrage of karma are all a
play of the Shakti as this world. You are that
peaceful, unblemished and Infinite
Consciousness that is both the cause and the
effect of these.

Contemplation 139
All that manifests in this world-appearance is
your reflection, the gold of your very own Self.
How could bracelets, armlets and anklets be
different from the gold they are made of?

Contemplation 140
Surrender all distinctions such as "I am this," "I
am not that." Recognize everything and everyone
as your very own Self and be happy.

Contemplation 141
It is through your ignorance that you have come
to believe that people, places and things are
different and separate from you. You are God and
God alone exists. Therefore, nothing exists that is
apart from you.

Contemplation 142
Knowing that this world appearance is an
imaginary play of the Shakti, become free of
limiting desire and craving and be at peace.

Contemplation 143
God alone exists and you are That. When you are not bound, what need is there of liberation? Understanding this, be happy.

Contemplation 144
You are pure Consciousness. Do not disturb your mind with thoughts of praise and blame. Be at peace and remain happily in the Self, the essence of Joy.

Contemplation 145
Recognizing that God alone exists, and that your thoughts are reflections of the Self – like ripples of waves on the ocean, don't let your mind hold on to anything.

Chapter 16

Ashtavakra continues to share his wisdom and instruction. The following contemplations are based on that instruction.

Contemplation 146
You may know and recite countless scriptures, but you will not be established within until you are unaffected by events, whether pleasant or unpleasant. The ability to forget everything and remain detached is the highest state possible.

Contemplation 147
As long as you follow the leadership and instruction of a Siddha Guru for your permanent spiritual transformation and Liberation, you may be learned, financially wealthy and active in worldly activities. These will not deter your mind from longing for that which is the cessation of desire, and beyond all goals.

Contemplation 148
You are the cause of your suffering. Realize this now and attain tranquility.

Contemplation 149
Happiness belongs only to that one who sees God in everything and everyone, everywhere.

Contemplation 150
When your mind is freed from chasing after pleasure in an attempt to avoid pain and you have risen above praise and blame you will be unattached to the body, mind and senses. You

will realize that Goad alone exists.

Contemplation 151
Be free of both attachment and aversion (the pair of opposites) to people, places and things. Then you will come to know your true nature.

Contemplation 152
So long as you engage in limiting desire and craving for people, places and things, you will lack discernment of the Truth. Then you will remain in the prison of attachment and aversion which are the foundation for death and rebirth.

Contemplation 153
Attachment and aversion are like two sides of the same coin. Pursuing one always leads to the pursuit of the other. When you are free of this pair of opposites, only then can you become established in the indescribable Joy of the Self.

Contemplation 154
While pursuing pleasure, a passionate person wants to be rid of the bondage of worldliness so as to avoid pain. Whereas as a dispassionate person is free from both pleasure and pain and does not recognize either.

Contemplation 155
The person who is proud about his/her spiritual progress while continuing to believe that he is the body, the mind and the senses continues to suffer the bondage of worldliness.

Contemplation 156
If even Shiva, Vishnu or the lotus-born Brahma were to lead you, until you are able to forget

everything and remain content in the Self, you are not freed from the bondage of worldliness.

Chapter 17

Ashtavakra continues to share his wisdom and instruction. The following contemplations are based on that instruction.

Contemplation 157
The one who is content in the solitude of the Self is able to purify the senses. Such a person gains the direct knowledge and experience of the Self. This is Yoga.

Contemplation 158
In the experience that God alone exists, one becomes a knower of the Truth. Then such a being sees God in everything and everyone, everywhere and is never distressed by daily, mundane activities.

Contemplation 159
Once you become absorbed in the Self, you are able to surrender your attachment to the body, mind and senses.

Contemplation 160
The person who is not attached to the things he has enjoyed and does not pursue the things he has not yet enjoyed is freed of the bondage of sense pleasures and worldly pleasures.

Contemplation 161
In this world-appearance, there are those who want to pursue pleasure in an attempt to avoid pain, and then there are those who have given up

this pursuit. The difference in the two is that the one who has given up the pursuit of pleasure and pain is able to rest in the indescribable Joy of the Self.

Contemplation 162
When the mind and heart are purified, you are free from attachment and aversion to religion, spirituality, financial wealth, sensuality and the notions of life and death.

Contemplation 163
A being who has surrender both attachment and aversion embraces this world-appearance as a play of the Shakti as this world and lives joyfully.

Contemplation 164
Fulfilled through knowledge of the Self, having made the restless mind quiet, you are able to live happily in this world-appearance, while fully engaged in your daily, mundane activities.

Contemplation 165
By way of the Love, Grace and Blessings of a Siddha Guru, you are released from the contraction of worldliness. Then you are able to rise above attachment and aversion and your senses can no longer disrupt your experience of the indescribable Joy of the Self.

Contemplation 166
Absorbed in the Self, you are able to see God in everything and everyone, everywhere. You are freed from the false notions of duality and diversity.

Contemplation 167
The one who is Liberated sees himself in everything, everywhere. Such a being is pure of heart.

Contemplation 168
A knower of the Truth, while seeing, hearing, feeling, smelling, tasting, speaking and walking about or sleeping, experiences only God in everything. Such a being has no desire to possess people, places and things or outcomes and is free.

Contemplation 169
For a liberated one there is no limiting desire or craving. Such a being neither blames, praises, rejoices, is disappointed, gives nor takes.

Contemplation 170
A Liberated one is elated at being unattached to people, places and things. Such a being does not fear death either, knowing that death does not exist. This being is truly Liberated.

Contemplation 171
For a Liberated one there is no distinction between pleasure and pain, man and woman, success and failure. Such a one experiences all these being equal in God and lives in a state of Equality Consciousness.

Contemplation 172
Being released from samsara by the Grace of a Siddha Guru, all confusion ends, and you experience Grace, Love and Light everywhere.

Contemplation 173
In the state of Liberation, you are able to express the fullness of humanity in an increasing state of delight in the inner Self. You are able to experience Joy, regardless of circumstance, discarding the notions of gain and loss.

Contemplation 174
Once established in the Self, the mind becomes still, like a flame where there is no wind. In this state the false notions of duality and diversity disappear.

Contemplation 175
Free from notions of "me" and "mine," free from attachment and aversion, being fully aware that everything here is a play of the Shakti, you experience non-action in the midst of activity, knowing that God is the one who acts.

Contemplation 176
By reining in the restless mind and causing it to dissolve in the indescribable Joy of the Self, you free yourself from delusion and the ignorance of worldliness.

Chapter 18

Ashtavakra continues to share his wisdom and instruction. The following contemplations are based on that instruction.

Contemplation 177
I praise the awareness of the Absolute that shatters the dross of worldly delusion and brings the experience of happiness, peace, love and light.

Contemplation 178
One must understand the difference between happiness and satisfaction. You may be satisfied by acquiring pleasure from objects (people, places and things), but you can only be happy by surrendering your attachment to objects and renouncing the limitation of the ego.

Contemplation 179
There is no happiness in doership. Happiness comes to one who resides in the supreme Joy of the Self, the Universal Experient that is both the cause and the effect.

Contemplation 180
This existence is imaginary. Apart from it there is only the Absolute that is beyond both being and non-being.

Contemplation 181
The experience of your God-nature, your oneness with God is inherent in your recognition that God alone exists in the myriad of forms and

is without beginning or end, unchanging and spotless.

Contemplation 182
By eliminating the delusion of worldliness and recognizing your God-nature, your ignorance is removed, and you live free from sorrow.

Contemplation 183
Understand that this world of forms is imaginary and that you are the Self, eternally free. Then you will stop behaving like a fool.

Contemplation 184
Knowing yourself to be God and understanding that both being and non-being are imaginary, become free of limiting desire and craving.

Contemplation 185
Considerations like "I am this" or "I am not this" no longer exist for the yogi who has gone silent realizing "Everything is my very own Self."

Contemplation 186
Find peace right where it is, inside yourself. Then you will not be distracted by knowledge or ignorance, pleasure or pain.

Contemplation 187
Once you are free from distinctions, free of the notions of duality and diversity, free of the notion of differences, knowing there is no such thing as gain or loss, then you may live anywhere and you will be joyful and at peace.

Contemplation 188
For one who is free from the pair of opposites, pleasure and pain, and free of the notion "I am

the doer," worldly existence becomes a paradise of non-attachment.

Contemplation 189
For the one who is liberated while still in the body, there is no attachment or aversion. For such a being the only thing left to be done is to follow God's will.

Contemplation 190
For one who is liberated while still in the body God alone exists and there is no outer world.

Contemplation 191
For one who lives in the state of desirelessness, such a being sees only God in everything and everyone, everywhere.

Contemplation 192
For the liberated sage, there is not even enough room to say, "I am God."

Contemplation 193
In the state of Liberation nothing can interrupt the experience of the indescribable Joy of the Self and there are no distractions.

Contemplation 194
Wisdom comes with not finding fault and not criticizing, condemning or complaining. In this way you are able to be in the world without being of the world.

Contemplation 195
For one who is immersed in the Self, free from limiting desire and craving and completely content, nothing actually takes place, even though such a being appears to act.

Contemplation 196
The wise person who just goes on doing what
presents itself to be done, encounters no
difficulty in either activity or inactivity.

Contemplation 197
The one who is free from limiting desire and
craving, self-reliant, independent and free of the
bondage of ignorance experiences non-action in
the midst of activity. Such a being is a servant of
God's will.

Contemplation 198
There is no suffering, no sadness and no sorrow
for one who has transcended samsara. Such a
being dwells in that state that is beyond the
mind, the body and the senses – eternally free.

Contemplation 199
Once you know, from direct experience, that the
indescribable Joy of the Self exists within you,
peace and purity shine in your being and there is
no need to renounce the world and no sense of
loss in anything.

Contemplation 200
When you empty your mind and conquer
restlessness, you will be able to surrender the
limitation of the ego by engaging humility,
reverence and longing for God and the Guru.

Contemplation 201
When your mind is empty of restlessness and
focused on the Self, you are able to surrender the
limitation of the ego. Then your daily mundane
activities become a blessed sacrament to God.

Contemplation 202
Once the ego idea is obliterated you experience that there is only one doer, that Universal Experient, God.

Contemplation 203
Performing your daily mundane activities as an offering, a blessed sacrament to God and the Guru, you come to know God's will for your life and are blessed.

Contemplation 204
When you are free of fear, doubt, worry and restlessness, you experience peace in the knowledge that it is God who experiences through your mind, body and senses – that God that you are.

Contemplation 205
Where there is no bondage, there is no need of liberation. When your mind is silent and you are immersed in the indescribable Joy of the Self, you are able to recognize everything as a play of the Shakti as this world.

Contemplation 206
The false sense of doership is the root cause of ignorance. When your attachment to expectations and wanting to control outcomes is destroyed, then you will realize that there is nothing to be gained or lost.

Contemplation 207
Once liberated, you rise above the notions of pleasure and pain and become unmoving, desireless and free from doubt.

Contemplation 208
Perform true meditation on the Self. Then all objects in your mind will dissolve and your mind itself will dissolve.

Contemplation 209
Only one who has cultivated humility, reverence and longing for God can recognize the truth that God alone exists.

Contemplation 210
Recognize all thoughts as manifesting by the Self, being sustained by the Self and then withdrawn by the Self. Observe the activity of your mind passively in this way, as a witness. Then you will experience peace, even in the midst of thinking.

Contemplation 211
There is no peace or happiness for one who is unaware of God within and everywhere.

Contemplation 212
You cannot come to know your God nature by thinking. It is only through the cessation of all thought that God is realized in the moment, from moment to moment.

Contemplation 213
Without the Grace, Blessings and leadership of a Siddha Guru it is impossible to attain permanent spiritual transformation and Liberation.

Contemplation 214
Permanent spiritual transformation cannot be attained through limiting desire and craving for this and that. It is only through the cessation of these that you can recognize God in everything and everyone, everywhere.

Contemplation 215
You cannot be freed from samsara without a fervent longing to know God, coupled with the Grace, Blessings and leadership of a Sadguru.

Contemplation 216
Peace does not come just because you say you want peace. A daily spiritual practice is required that is instructed by a Siddha Guru.

Contemplation 217
Direct knowledge of the Self is not an intellectual understanding. This knowledge only comes by way of the experience of going beyond the mind, beyond the body and beyond the senses to that Witness to your mind.

Contemplation 218
The restless mind can only be calmed through direct experience of the indescribable Joy of the Self.

Contemplation 219
God alone exists and there is no outer world. Understanding this, seek God right where God is within yourself.

Contemplation 220
The only way to know God is to have a growing, direct experience of the indescribable Joy of the Self. This experience comes through vigilant, daily spiritual practice as instructed by a Siddha Guru.

Contemplation 221
Permanent spiritual transformation and Liberation cannot be attained through thinking,

nor through mere belief. This state is only
attained by resting in the inner Self.

Contemplation 222
Those who are unaware of the Truth seek refuge
by abandoning their worldly, mundane
responsibilities and seeking solitude away from
interaction with people, places and things.

Contemplation 223
Truly, what is to be abandoned is the limitation
of the ego and limiting desire and craving for this
and that. In this way, you are no longer a slave to
your senses.

Contemplation 224
The one whose mind is quiet and free from
doubts can experience Liberation in the moment,
from moment to moment, even in the midst of
daily mundane activities.

Contemplation 225
The one whose mind is pure, who is not
distracted by worldliness and remains absorbed
in the Self, does not act, even though appearing
to do so.

Contemplation 226
By following God's Will, which is nothing other
than the Guru's Will, you are able to take full
responsibility for your daily mundane activities
without taint.

Contemplation 227
By the Bliss of the Self one attains happiness, by
the Bliss of the Self one reaches the Supreme, by
the Bliss of the Self one comes to absence of

thought, by the Bliss of the Self one recognizes the Ultimate Reality.

Contemplation 228
When you come to know that you are not the doer and outcomes do not belong to you, but to God, then your mind will be content with being at peace.

Contemplation 229
By making every action a blessed sacrament to God you are able to surrender the notion of doership in the indescribable Joy of the Self.

Contemplation 230
Once you have conquered your restless mind and are able to rest in the Self, you will enjoy living anywhere.

Contemplation 231
Immersed in God, knowers of the Truth have no attachment and no aversion to anything or anyone.

Contemplation 232
A yogi is one who, by way of the instruction of a living Sadguru, is able to rise above both praise and blame.

Contemplation 233
A yogi is one who, by way of the instruction of a living Sadguru, is able to extinguish the fires of pleasure and pain in the Bliss of the Self.

Contemplation 234
The notion that you are just the mind, the body and the senses, and that you must possess

outcomes to be somebody is the cause of
samsara. Liberation is its opposite.

Contemplation 235
When your mind is restless, you are agitated
even when doing nothing. When your mind is
quiet, you experience peace even when engaged
in daily mundane activities.

Contemplation 236
Being at peace, you are able to experience the
indescribable Joy of the Self whether speaking,
standing, sitting, walking, eating, sleeping or
engaged in any other activity.

Contemplation 237
The one who experiences only Joy while going
about daily mundane activities remains
undisturbed by situations and circumstances of
any kind.

Contemplation 238
To abstain from action without addressing the
restless mind is foolish. When the mind is quiet
and absorbed in God, seeing everything as a play
of the Shakti, action becomes non-action.

Contemplation 239
When you destroy attachment and aversion to
people, places and things you are able to interact
without contracting. Then, whether you have few
possessions or a lot of possessions, neither can
bind you.

Contemplation 240
It is the nature of the mind to think. When you
quiet your restless mind and turn it within you

realize that, when there is nothing that needs to be done, you can stop thinking.

Contemplation 241
Perform your daily mundane activities with one-pointedness, and without expectations or the desire to possess outcomes. Then you will be able to destroy attachment and aversion.

Contemplation 242
See God in everything and everyone. Then, even in the midst of activity, you will be able to reduce everything and everyone to sameness with God. In this way, your mind will become free of limiting desire and craving.

Contemplation 243
You are so much greater than you think you are. To free yourself from samsara you must destroy the false notion of individuality that has you believing that you are just the mind, just the body and the senses.

Contemplation 244
By abandoning your attachment to outcomes and your desire to possess people, places and things, you are able to remain content in the experience of turning your mind within to the glory of the inner Self.

Contemplation 245
When you destroy your union with pleasure and pain, it is an easy matter to surrender your attachments and aversions. This the only way to freedom.

Contemplation 246
Once you have abandoned the ego idea, your attachments and aversions are burned in the fire of your love for God and the Guru. Then there is nothing else to be done.

Contemplation 247
By way of the uninterrupted experience of the indescribable Joy of the Self, you become pure and at peace. Then you are able to see the play of the Shakti as this world.

Contemplation 248
As you are transformed from within through the ongoing experience of the Self, you realize that God alone exists.

Contemplation 249
For one who is established in the Self, realizing God, there is neither pleasure or pain and neither bondage or liberation.

Contemplation 250
Samsara remains until God-realization. Once God-realized, one lives in a state of total freedom, unattached to outcomes.

Contemplation 251
Having merged in God, you rise above body consciousness and remain free of limiting desire and craving. You see only God in everything and everyone, everywhere.

Contemplation 252
Attempting to give up thinking is futile. Instead, think of nothing but the Absolute. This is how to purify the mind and make it golden.

Contemplation 253
You are not freed from the illusion of worldliness by simply hearing of the Truth. A firm, vigilant, daily spiritual practice as instructed by a living Sadguru is the only means to free yourself from the prison of worldliness.

Contemplation 254
Although appearing to be active, one who has merged in the inner Self does nothing.

Contemplation 255
One who is established in the Self is fearless and unmoved by pleasure and pain, praise and blame. For such a being God alone exists and there is no outer world.

Contemplation 256
When you realize your oneness with God, you are freed from the false identity of individuality, freed from the notion that you are just a person.

Contemplation 257
For the Liberated God alone exists and there is no such thing as a separate world. For such a being everything is the praise and worship of the Lord.

Contemplation 258
Filled with the indescribable Joy of the Self, you realize there is no such thing as gain or loss.

Contemplation 259
One who is immersed in the inner Self experiences Vairagya, elated dispassion. Being elated at being non-attached, there is no praise or blame of anything or anyone. The mind rests in Equality Consciousness.

Contemplation 260
Filled with the wisdom of God, Samsara is
destroyed, and you consider all actions you
perform to be non-action.

Contemplation 261
Filled with the wisdom of God, all expectations
are dashed and attachment and aversion,
pleasure and pain – these dissolve in the Bliss of
the Absolute.

Contemplation 262
Filled with the wisdom of God, you know only
peace and are able to see the play of the Shakti as
this world everywhere and in everything.

Contemplation 263
When immersed in the Self, body consciousness
dissolves in the recognition of the Absolute.

Contemplation 264
Filled with the wisdom of God, you are freed
from the notions of duality and diversity. Rid of
all doubts, you rest in the Joy of non-attachment.

Contemplation 265
Filled with the wisdom of God, you are freed
from all sense of being just the body, the mind
and the senses. The knot of the heart is cut away
and you are freed of limiting desire and craving.

Contemplation 266
Upon the dawning of Liberation, you become
content with being content.

Contemplation 267
Only the one immersed in the Self knows without

knowing, sees without seeing and speaks without speaking.

Contemplation 268
Immersed in the Self, you conquer limiting desire and craving and rise above the notions of "good" and "bad."

Contemplation 269
Immersed in the Self, you rise above both virtue and vice. Armed with Viveka, you become pure and sincere.

Contemplation 270
The indescribable Joy of the Self makes you desireless and free.

Contemplation 271
One who is Liberated experiences the Bliss of the Self at all times, in waking, in meditation and even in deep sleep. Such a being is always awake and aware.

Contemplation 272
For one who is immersed in the Self, there is only the play of the Shakti as this world and God alone exists.

Contemplation 273
An enjoyer of the Bliss of the Absolute is neither happy or sad and remains elated at being unattached to people, places and things.

Contemplation 274
When you rein in your restless mind it becomes still, like a flame where there is no wind.

Contemplation 275
For one who is Liberated, there is no attachment
to outcomes, no expectations of this and that,
and no greed.

Contemplation 276
A Liberated one has risen above praise and
blame and has no fear of death. Such a being is
free attachment and aversion.

Contemplation 277
Once you are at peace, there is no need to run off
to popular places and no need to flee from the
world. You see God in everything and everyone,
everywhere.

Chapter 19

Upon hearing the utterances of Ashtavakra, Janaka continues to share his realization of the Truth. The following contemplations are based on that.

Contemplation 278
Using the tweezers of the direct knowledge of the Self, I have managed to extract the painful thorn of endless opinions from the recesses of my heart.

Contemplation 279
Established in the glory of my God nature, there is no longer any path to follow, no philosophy to embrace and no duality or diversity either.

Contemplation 280
Established in the glory of my God nature, time no longer exists and there is the realization that this world is a prolonged dream.

Contemplation 281
Established in the glory of my God nature, there is no good or evil and I am fully present with God, whether thinking or not.

Contemplation 282
Established in the glory of my God nature, there is no waking, no dreaming, no deep sleep and no fear.

Contemplation 283
Established in the glory of my God nature, there

is no separate world. There is only God.

Contemplation 284
Established in the glory of my God nature, death
no longer exists, and life is an expression of
God's nature.

Contemplation 285
Remaining immersed in the Self, all my seeking
has come to an end.

Chapter 20

Upon hearing the utterances of Ashtavakra, Janaka continues to share his realization of the Truth. The following contemplations are based on that.

Contemplation 286
Having merged in God, I see only God everywhere.

Contemplation 287
Having merged in God, there is no duality, no diversity and no separation. There is no longer a need for scriptures and nothing to free myself from.

Contemplation 288
Having merged in God, there is no longer any such thing as knowledge or ignorance, no bondage, no liberation and no outer world.

Contemplation 289
Freed from the false notion of individuality, you merge in the Ultimate Reality, the Self. Then there is no death or rebirth for you.

Contemplation 290
Freed from the false notion of individuality, you conquer doership by surrendering the limitation of the ego in your direct experience of the Ultimate Reality, the Self.

Contemplation 291
Upon Self-realization, you realize that there is no

outer world and God alone exists.

Contemplation 292
Upon Self-realization, there is nothing else to attain, no pleasure and no pain, and no gain or loss.

Contemplation 293
Immersed in the state of Supreme Shiva, you become a knower of the Truth. You realize that this world-appearance is neither real or unreal, that it is a reflection of the Bliss of the inner Self.

Contemplation 294
Immersed in the state of Supreme Shiva, you experience that there is no sorrow, no suffering and no sadness. You experience that everything is a play of the Shakti.

Contemplation 295
Immersed in the state of Supreme Shiva, you are forever pure. Then, for you there is no samsara, no attachment or aversion and no illusion of any kind.

Contemplation 296
Immersed in the inner Self, you become unmovable and indivisible. Then there is no such thing as activity or inactivity.

Contemplation 297
Immersed in the inner Self, you live without limitation in the direct experience of the Absolute.

Contemplation 298
Immersed in the inner Self, there is no longer being or non-being, no duality or diversity – just God.

About Nityananda Shaktipat Yoga

Love is the highest religion, the greatest spiritual path of humankind. Therefore, we welcome you with Love, we Honor you and we Respect you. In addition, our path of worship and study is led by Kedarji. He is a Sadguru (meaning true spiritual leader), holistic practitioner/researcher and natural healing scientist who has a reputation for leading without insisting that people follow. To this end, here you will experience programs that embody worship through meditation, chanting, prayer, contemplation and the study of scriptures/sacred texts. We are a non-denominational sanctuary of worship open to people of all paths and faiths.

For more information about programs, events, courses and retreats to strengthen the practices and awareness spoken of in this book visit

NityanandaShaktipatYoga.Org

RECOMMENDED FURTHER READING

The Verses On Witness Consciousness by Kedarji
https://www.nityanandashaktipatyoga.org/boo
ks-on-meditation-the-verses-on-witness-
consciousness/

Vibration of Divine Consciousness. A Spiritual Autobiography – by Kedarji

https://www.nityanandashaktipatyoga.org/boo
ks-on-self-realization-vibration-of-divine-
consciousness/

Websites

BhagawanNityananda.org
NityanandaShaktipatYoga.org
ShaktipatBlessing.org

.

www.ingramcontent.com/pod-product-compliance
Lightning Source LLC
Chambersburg PA
CBHW061712120626
46550CB00003B/1189